W9-BZC-054

Wheelchair Sports
at the Paralympics

BY MATT BOWERS

Amicus High Interest is published by Amicus and Amicus Ink
P.O. Box 1329, Mankato, MN 56002
www.amicuspublishing.us

Copyright © 2020 Amicus. International copyright reserved in
all countries. No part of this book may be reproduced in any
form without written permission from the publisher.

Library of Congress Cataloging-in-Publication Data
Names: Bowers, Matt, author.
Title: Wheelchair sports at the Paralympics / by Matt Bowers.
Description: Mankato, Minnesota : Amicus | Amicus Ink,
  [2020] | Series: Paralympic Sports | Audience: Grades: K to
  Grade 3. | Includes webography. | Includes index.
Identifiers: LCCN 2018051706 (print) | LCCN 2018055073
  (ebook) | ISBN 9781681518671 (pdf) | ISBN
  9781681518275 (Library Binding) | ISBN
  9781681525556 (Paperback)
Subjects: LCSH: Paralympics—Juvenile literature. | Wheelchair
  sports—Juvenile literature. | Sports for people with disabilities—
  Juvenile literature.
Classification: LCC GV722.5.P37 (ebook) | LCC
  GV722.5.P37 B68 2020 (print) | DDC 796.04/56—dc23
LC record available at https://lccn.loc.gov/2018051706

Editor: Alissa Thielges
Series Designer: Kathleen Petelinsek
Book Designer: Ciara Beitlich
Photo Researchers: Holly Young and Shane Freed

Photo Credits: AP/Kyodo cover; AP/Jens Büttner 5;
Shutterstock/A.RICARDO 6; Newscom/Bob Daemmrich 9;
Getty/Kay Nietfeld/picture alliance 10–11; AP/Leo Correa
12, 19, 26; AP/Elizabeth Dalziel 15; Newscom/Adam Davy
16; WikiMedia Commons/Agência Brasil Fotografias 20–21;
Alamy/Nippon News 22; Getty/Thomas Lovelock for OIS/
IOC/AFP 25; Alamy/Andrew Matthews 29

Printed in the United States of America

HC 10 9 8 7 6 5 4 3 2 1
PB 10 9 8 7 6 5 4 3 2 1

Table of Contents

Going for Gold   4

Wheelchair Basketball   7

Wheelchair Tennis   13

Wheelchair Rugby   18

Wheelchair Fencing   24

The Next Paralympics   28

Glossary   30

Read More   31

Websites   31

Index   32

Going for Gold

It's the Summer Paralympic Games! Here athletes with a **disability** compete in Olympic-style games. They come from around the world. They are ready to go for the gold.

The first Paralympic Games took place in 1960. Wheelchair sports were some of the first sports played. Wheelchairs help people with limited mobility compete.

 When and where do the Paralympic Games take place?

Clodoaldo Silva lights the fire to start the 2016 Paralympics.

 The Paralympics are two weeks after the summer and winter Olympics. They take place in the same host city.

A player from Turkey makes a
shot in a game against the U.S.

Wheelchair Basketball

Athletes in wheelchairs zoom down a basketball court. They dash and spin. Teammates pass the ball. One player shoots. The ball flies through the air. Swish! Two points!

Wheelchair basketball is an action-packed team sport. Each team has five players on the court. They work together to score the most points.

Wheelchair basketball is like basketball. The court is the same size. The rules are similar, too. The player with the ball can't **travel**. They can push their wheels twice before they must **dribble**, pass, or shoot. If they don't, the other team gets the ball. Players can't run into other wheelchairs on the court. This is a **foul**.

 In wheelchair basketball, what is the height of the basket?

 The basket height is 10 feet (3 m) above the court, just like in basketball.

The chairs in wheelchair basketball are made for the sport. They are light and strong. The wheels angle out. This helps the players make tight turns. It also makes the chair more stable.

At the first Paralympics, only men played wheelchair basketball. In 1968, women's teams began to compete. In 2016, both the men's and women's U.S. teams won gold medals.

The U.S. women's team celebrates winning gold in the 2016 Paralympics.

Wheelchair Tennis

A wheelchair tennis player tosses the tennis ball into the air. She swings her **racket**. The ball rockets over the net. Her competitor goes for the ball. Smack! The ball zooms back over the net. This is wheelchair tennis! Tennis wheelchairs are nimble and fast. They help the players move quickly around the court.

Diede de Groot from the Netherlands serves the ball.

Wheelchair tennis and tennis have a lot in common. Both use the same court. The rackets and balls are the same, too. One difference is the two-bounce rule. The ball can bounce twice before a player must hit it back over the net. If it bounces a third time, the opponent scores a point.

 Are there any other differences between wheelchair tennis and tennis?

Great Britain and Sweden play for gold in the men's finals in 2008.

 In wheelchair tennis, the ball can land outside the court on the second bounce and remain in play.

Alfie Hewett and Gordon Reid of Great Britain play doubles tennis in 2016.

 Do all wheelchair athletes have to use a wheelchair in their daily lives?

Game! Set! **Match**! Wheelchair tennis is made up of these three things. Matches are the ultimate win. They are made up of 3 sets of 6 games. Whoever wins the most sets, wins the match.

Players compete in singles and doubles. In singles, two players face off. In doubles, two teams of two compete.

 No. Players only need to have a disability that affects their movement.

Wheelchair Rugby

Crash! Two wheelchairs collide. The players fight for the ball. One gains control and passes it to a teammate. She weaves down the court. Score! Wheelchair rugby is a team sport. There are 12 players on a team. They can be both men and women. Four players from each team play on the court at a time.

Australian Ryley Batt (yellow) fights for the ball against a British player.

Wheelchair rugby is a **contact sport**. Players run into each other a lot. Special wheelchairs were made for this sport. The **offense** uses a smaller wheelchair. It is designed to go fast and turn easily. The **defense** uses a chair with a long front bumper. It is built to stop players on the other team.

A player holds the ball in his lap as he dodges his opponents.

France plays Japan in wheelchair rugby at the 2016 Paralympics.

 Who won the gold medal in wheelchair rugby at the 2016 Paralympic Games?

Wheelchair rugby is played on an indoor court. It is the size of a basketball court. At each end of the court, two cones mark the goal line. Players must carry the ball over that line to score. Teams work together. They pass, dribble, and roll the ball. They move toward the goal line.

 Australia. USA won silver and Japan won bronze.

Wheelchair Fencing

Two fencers face off. Their wheelchairs are fixed to the ground. The chairs can't move. They wear special protective gear. "En garde," says the referee. The fencers bring their blades up. "Ready? Play!" The **bout** begins. The athletes lunge. They try to hit each other. Wheelchair fencing takes great skill and speed.

Wheelchair fencers stay in one place. They use their upper body to compete.

Protective gear keeps two fencers safe in a sabre event.

 How do the judges know when the blade has touched a fencer?

Wheelchair fencing has three events: foil, épée, and sabre. The difference is the type of blade used. In each event, players score a point when their blade touches the other player's upper body. Fencers wear a lot of protective gear. A mask protects the face. Gloves are used to cover the hands. And a heavy jacket protects the rest of the body.

A fencer's gear has sensors. When a hit lands, a scoreboard shows the point.

The Next Paralympics

Athletes who play wheelchair sports show incredible strength, skill, and teamwork. The Paralympics has many sports for wheelchair athletes. Para athletics, archery and cycling are just a few examples. In 2020, badminton will be added to the Paralympics. Wheelchairs can be used in this sport, too. Tune in to watch!

 Where will the 2020 Paralympic Games be played?

Singles tennis players celebrate winning the gold, silver, and bronze medals in the 2016 Paralympics.

 In 2020, the Summer Paralympic Games will be held in Tokyo, Japan.

Glossary

bout In fencing, a contest between two fencers.

contact sport A sport where players come into physical contact with one another.

defense The players who defend the goal against the other team.

disability A physical or mental condition that limits a person's movements, senses, or activities.

dribble To bounce a basketball off the ground.

foul An action in a sport that is against the rules and results in a penalty for the team whose player made the foul.

match In wheelchair tennis, a match is made up of 3 sets of 6 games. To win a match, a player or team must win 2 of the 3 sets.

offense The players who are trying to score.

racket Sports equipment with a handle and a round or oval frame with a tight netting, like nylon, stretched across it, used for striking a ball.

travel In wheelchair basketball, when a player fails to dribble the ball after pushing their wheelchair forward more than two times.

Read More

Fullman, Joe. *Going for Gold: A Guide to the Summer Games*. London: Wayland, 2016.

Osborne, M. K. *Basketball*. Mankato, Minn.: Amicus, 2020.

Websites

International Wheelchair Basketball Foundation
https://iwbf.org/

Olympics | Paralympic Games: History
https://www.olympic.org/paralympic-games

Paralympics | Sports
https://www.paralympic.org/sports/summer

Every effort has been made to ensure that these websites are appropriate for children. However, because of the nature of the Internet, it is impossible to guarantee that these sites will remain active indefinitely or that their contents will not be altered.

Index

2020 Paralympics 28–29

basketball 7–10
  basket height 8–9

court sizes 8, 14, 23

fencing 24–27
  protective gear 24, 27
  scoring 26–27

gold medals 4, 10, 22

history 4, 10, 22–23

rugby 18–23
  defense 21
  offense 21

tennis 13–17
  doubles 17
  singles 17
  two-bounce rule 14

wheelchair adaptions
  10, 13, 21, 24

wheelchair rules 8–9,
  14–15, 16–17, 24

About the Author

Matt Bowers is a writer and illustrator who lives in Minnesota. When he's not writing or drawing, he enjoys skiing, sailing, and going on adventures with his family. As a sports fan, he looks forward to the 2020 Paralympic Games in Tokyo, Japan!